Made in the USA
Monee, IL
21 May 2020

31627294R00072